Coyote Logic

Coyote Logic

poems

LISA DOMINGUEZ ABRAHAM

Blue Oak Press
Rocklin | California

Cover design by Maxima Kahn
Cover painting: *Coyotl – Urban Coyote*
Copyright © by Monica Aissa Martinez
Interior design by Sarah Miner·
Typeset in Centaur

Printed and bound by Bookmobile
Printed in the United States

Library of Congress Cataloging-in-Publication Data
Abraham, Lisa Dominguez
Coyote Logic: poems by Lisa Dominguez Abraham

ISBN 978-0-9975040-1-9

CONTENTS

I

II

III

I

God Poured Voice

God poured voice in me, a woman-shaped bowl,
then skimmed a finger along the rim

until I hummed. I was set down,
a bowl of breath and space in Eden's green

and though Adam's skin at daybreak glowed
like home, I couldn't rest, and restless

sought the apple tree, blossoms unfolding
into fruit, the apples kin to stars

speeding from Big Bang. I hungered for surge,
a straight shot to the unknown

and bit through, juice bathing my vocal cords,
my voice no longer God's alone.

The Axial Tilt of Earth

Like everyone, I follow directives below recognition
until I arrive in a roomful of strangers

who have dyed their hair
and carefully shopped for workout pants,

a gym where the metallic fragrance
of hand weights expands behind my eyes

and scent becomes sound. The air rings
with Beyoncé's affirmations as I watch myself

lift reps in time with the other women,
apparently solid though I'm pierced

by texts and calls through each cell.
This is how I live most days, unaware

of solar wind and the earth's axial tilt.
Our teacher is grey-haired

and strong. She nods to the music,
shows us how rhythm increases

the body's telepathy until we move in synch.
And though each woman arrived separately,

together we face the huge gym mirror,
lifting and lowering outstretched arms.

Emigration

Last week I scrubbed yellow shadows
from my bedroom wall, erasing
the last traces of wedding pictures
carefully stored away.

For a moment, emptiness felt clean.
But each night as my children
turn through sleep, I dream:

I am my grandmother raising a lantern
as she crosses a stubble field in Zacatecas
to bargain with a ghost for silver.
It's 1914. Soldiers have slaughtered
all her chickens, sliced the corn field with bayonets.
Her daughters shiver in the barn and I'm frightened
feeling my legs in her skirts
until courage contracts
to a metallic taste on my tongue.
Coiled around a filthy sack
in a shallow cave, the ghost lets me
grab one handful of coins

and I wake gripping my own thumbs.
Guitarróns thrum from the clock radio.
On folded newspapers, three paint cans.

I'll pry open the lids,
stir lilac, white, and green,
then paint my walls with pictographs—
a band of women traveling
toward a country they've never seen.

On Seeing a Family Cemetery

We who descend from refugees—
quick moves and no money,
only ache packed from place to place—
our dead could be anywhere,
scattered graves,
the scattered pollen of ash.
Removed by just one generation
we meet only in séance
or dream, faces hazy
but the laughs familiar. Above,
strange flocks circle,
gaining the height to see
who they're meant to guide.
They have lost countries
but understand music,
sending down to us what they can,
the remembered notes of folksongs,
refrains fitted with wings.

Home Remedy

The wrinkled print of my mother's grip
branded my arm when she pulled me,
a toddler, from boiling water I spilled
as I tried to touch steam
rising from the stove.

Years later she said I was still trouble,
refusing dresses and barrettes. Normal girls whispered
about boys—I yodeled to neighborhood dogs,
leading my pack through vacant lots
until the day my throat swelled with strep
so sore I confessed and opened
my mouth to my mom.

She drove me to the railyard,
to a boxcar with wheels rusted fast
and a trellis of bougainvillea.
Inside she whispered Spanish
to an old woman who braced her palm
against my forehead, angled a stick

past my tongue to dab thick salt paste
onto tonsils. Saliva trickled
like broth through constriction, a treatment
to cure strep and perhaps rinse
my voice to a gentler tone.
They listened to me breathe,
eyes narrow, waiting.

Passing Through

I pull sheets from the queen in 303,
stoop for booze bottles and collapsed condoms—

we're not so ephemeral as some suppose.
Each day new guests delight

in taut sheets and little soaps,
this room a shimmer that will burst

forgotten upon checkout
along with all they leave behind—magic

in pared nails and stray hairs.
I'm here to sweep up and disinfect

the proof of lives passing through.
It's what they pay for, luggage gleaming

on stiff leashes they pull down the hall
as though there's no trail

of footprints in the carpet, no thumbprint
pressed in bathroom counter shine.

Coyote Logic

Be a woman, smiling. Wait
for your manager to wrap his story

before punching
the diner's time clock

for a double shift, the long trot.
Blend in. Cream with that?

And save untouched fries
on a forgotten shelf

of the walk-in. Cut small,
tossed with chili powder

and toasted, they'll be perfect
kid snacks. Friday night

hide the children under a blanket
on the backseat floor

of your Oldsmobile.
Shush them and pull forward

to pay for a single drive-in ticket
with your tips—all ones—

the movie, Pixar-something.
Park and let the kids scramble

over the front seat. Pass them
the greasy paper bag and watch

their faces as they savor each bite,
savor your tricks, how you

scavenge overlooked caches
for morsels of joy.

Las Brujas

For Q

You see us first as lit candles,
as flickers nestled in red roses
we pin in our hair,
then by the wavering glow
of white lace shawls, our full lace skirts
held out like fans. We turn a slow circle,
our skirts brushing one another,
dancing, candles balanced on our heads
at two in the morning.
Syncopated heel beats
draw you to us,
seven candles below
the expansive night sky,
below where you watch
our sparks rising
as you flicker high above.

Breadcrumbs

Not birds but a sculptor has gathered
Hansel and Gretel's breadcrumbs

and glued them into a tiny loaf of bread
strategically lit to glisten

as an art installation. He's also built
a drum kit from the towel-wrapped water jug

a teenager dropped as she made her way north
through dust and scorpions.

Art aficionados walk around the kit,
study an unknown girl's despair.

Some sense she makes it from Sinaloa
where teenagers wield guns

all the way to the candied land where she
sorts grapes for artists who make wine.

It's unclear which side of the border
is home or oven

as she stands beside other masked women,
quick hands working to send

whatever she can,
from a thin paycheck, south.

Return: Sunday Morning in Watts

There's the yard where Mom threw feed
to fierce *pollitos* raised to fight as cocks,
mad puffs, quick beaks that pecked her feet.

And from the hot pink house, *rancheras* trumpet
like they did when Rosa's 'uncles' visited
after church, one half hour at a time.

Mom takes my arm and we enter church,
the Mass intoned in Spanish, the same grim saints,
El Señor a manikin, his beard glued on imperfectly.

From there we stroll to her old school and she returns
the smiles of everyone, a woman in a hair net,
a junkie pedaling by. For once

an ocean breeze slips though the factories
that loom around this neighborhood.
Mom watches the poplar trees shimmy

and inhales air scented
just as she remembers, warm
and spiced with salt and balsam.

Hoodoos Will Appear Where You Are Standing

The ground feels solid as my own rib cage pressing into the rail that keeps me from the drop into the canyon. An information panel describes what will be here in the future—more sandstone spires as the canyon widens. I thought hoodoo meant the power to charm or curse, but here it testifies to what lasts.

From my mother's core,
though memory crumbles, her
laugh is strong and clear.

Seamstress

I.

No longer your daughter,
I've become a stranger
you confide in, whispering

> *I found quiet shadows*
> *under the tree that shakes the wind.*
> *I saved them someplace.*

Perhaps in the dresser you edit,
secretly tucking another shirt or sock
into the trash, creating

drawers of space where shadows
waver and shift. You study the floor,
its terra cotta tiles, grout lines

> *Here, between the US and Mexico*
> *is my home. Neighbors grow figs*
> *in their own little gardens. Each morning*
> *when they cross the border to work,*
> *policemen smile and wave.*

II.

My childhood was gold lamés,
pilled sweaters I picked through
whenever we scavenged Goodwill.

You rubbed fabric to check cotton or blend,
turned a blouse inside out
to gauge its seams. You could remove

bric-a-brac, broaden a sleeve.
Whatever I wanted
could be made more me.

When I was 16, I found a jeans jacket.
You called it too thin and told me to fish
the bargain bin. Sorting
soured T-shirts and misshapen skirts,
I pulled up a stained coat
lined in pristine yellow silk
you could scissor out
and stitch inside my choice.
You winked, Good job.

III.

You miss only the dead. Anxious
that your own mom is sick,
your father missing, you search the house

> *I left them in this room.*
> *No, this one.*

Memory's seamstress, I pick through
your stories for pieces
that fit this moment:

Picture Saturday nights. Your mom
sashays across the community center stage
in a cocktail dress she stitched
from the skirts of four old rayon aprons.
The dress is fitted, original.
Everyone quiets as she sings
"Estrellita" like a diva

and my dad, the best dancer,
salsas with her, then me,
then with all the pretty girls

And next door, the *curandera,*
and across the street

my best friend. We walk together
to our cannery shifts.
We make each other laugh.

I want to go home.

My hand on yours, I nod.
You'll be there soon.

Museum Security

Camouflaged in his navy blazer and dark skin,
my cousin blends into the display of Ancient Egypt

and steps from shadow only to say
Don't Touch or No Flash. In a glass box

a single cheek and pair of lips glisten.
Nefertiti—fragments of her.

He studies the broken edge
of brown stone and her polished mouth

as patrons wander by, eyes opaque
with the freedom to take in Egypt

and the Impressionists and a latte in one visit.
They stroll past the queen's curved mouth,

so perfect it sparks
a man's thirst for a lost world.

No Medal, No Parade

My nephew refuses
to lean out a car window
and shoot a passer-by,
the key to proving he's a soldier
tough enough to join the local crew.
Refuses
even after a lead pipe
smashes his temple.

The crew boss trusts
the snub-nosed pistol pressed
to the base of my nephew's skull,
the single bullet
in the chamber he spins
sending the message
that neither one knows
whether his squeeze
will bring a naked click.

My boy flinches when the trigger
does, in fact, click
but he spits each word—
Go ahead, motherfucker,
spin it again.

Closure

My uncle's card reads technician, not tailor,
an echo of his job in Mexico

as a civil engineer. He fixes mechanics'
ripped coveralls and toolbelts, piecing together

sections that don't fit neat, stitching
closures a working man trusts will last.

With no apprentice, his craft will end
in this small shop. But for now

Piolín cracks jokes on the radio
and Uncle grins sometimes as he reaches

into a tackle box of top stops and sliders
salvaged from jackets too thread-worn for Goodwill,

then rubs his thumb over the teeth of a zipper
made right, its links hooking smooth and tight.

Handmade Gifts

A necklace of flat bones and Chinese coins,
a Cost Plus amulet made in Taiwan

was placed in my hand while I still trembled
in post-op. In my haze I pictured

the roses patients get on TV, petals fragrant as skin.
Home from the hospital I dismantled the necklace

filling one bag with coins, another with bones
then lay in bed, teary from the stapled incision.

My cat, skittish and unable to meow,
crawled into the crook of my arm, having heard

the cry she'd make if she could, and I decided
to string those bones as wind chimes that would sing

to the two of us our little fears. Some gifts
suggest what might be ahead. Others

echo the past, like my vase that leans west.
A retired neighbor gave it to me as she whispered

that she survived Hiroshima—her insurance company
must never know. Now she takes Ceramics 101

for the sake of clay she shapes and glazes
mushroom brown, then decorates with a bamboo

pattern that imprints black inside the kiln.
Like it or not, she can't escape the motif:

mushroom and shadow. After all that heat,
the thin neck leans. She knows I don't mind.

She knows what I'm learning now.

II

Think Back

"We think back through our mothers if we are women."
   ~ Virginia Woolf

Neither wife nor maid, the witch read
books of subtle poisons

while I scrubbed other people's linens
and our one-room cottage floor,

working toward each twilight
when I could gaze over the garden wall

into her tangled plots of cabbages and herbs.
Intrigued, I hungered for her greens

and sent my husband to her
where he did my bidding

but promised the witch my womb.
Rapunzel grew into the girl

who was never mine. But when she began to toddle
through the witch's garden, I began again

to spy beyond my own walled yard,
watching the witch hunch into herself

as she approached the loss
she knew love would bring—

Rapunzel shorn and banished.

I heard that near a scruffy desert town
the girl set up shop, mixing potions for the locals

until her prince, blinded, stumbled into her again.
I heard they lived happily ever after

a privileged life, though his people
found her odd. She ate raw greens

and shunned palace luncheons
for a garden where she'd read

or kneel among rows of bush beans
with a shovel and a basket

and her twin little girls—one named Hazel,
after rumor of me.

The other, Gothel. After the witch.

Blue Corn Woman

(Based on a Huichol myth)

She slept by her sisters, Red Corn and Yellow Corn,
their dreams knotting into corn cobs they gave away
to polite ants, needy sparrows. Each day they played dress-up
and she fell for make-believe like every girl—
someday she'd have a husband, her cheek in the curve
between his shoulder and chest, like heaven, that myth
of both arrival and rest. But her mother sent her away
to save the village of Colotlán where children suffered
distended bellies and stick arms, sent her with a starving man
disguised as his bride.

Her mother warned her to keep it simple, to sit alone
each day gathering strength for sleep, to lay alone
each night so her dreams could bead into kernels—
violet, cream and inky black, a pile of cobs in the *zócolo*
the village would bless, a miracle. But from within her hut
she could hear other women call her the lazy girl,
too stuck-up to work. That's why, impatient and lonely,
she tried to prove herself with a wife's task—
pat *masa* into a tortilla, set it on the *comal*.

She forgot that her skin, being corn, would blister along fingertips,
up her arms. Her husband found her curled and burned,
human now. He let her stay until she healed
with crumpled skin that keeps sweat from trickling out
or dreams from seeping in. Now in Mazatlán she lives on a sidewalk
and twists together shoulder bags for tourists
as she strains each morning to hear her sisters' dreams—
from distant hills the rumble of red and yellow corn.
Even on a crowded street she hears silk tassels hiss.
She knows it's her sisters who send the breeze
that ruffles her hair, cools her cheek.

Iron Goddess of Mercy

sees the child hiding
between a mattress and box springs

as his mother smacks her belt against the wall
and screams what she'll do if she finds him.

The goddess finds her own small face
weighted, breathing dust

and sends him a faint note
of honeysuckle. He can scent it

eyes clenched. Years after his escape
he will plant that tangled vine

to remind himself of hope. And decades later
the goddess, being iron,

will allow her face to bend into
the mother's pinched expression

unfocused now. She will grant her
a cup of pale green tea,

a hint of honey and herb. And because the mother
has lost touch with everyone

she tried to care for, has lost even her rage,
the goddess will allow her to forget.

Pocket Litter

The salesman thinks just one more drink,
a mistake anyone could make.
But after the crash, no father cares.

He wants to know what was found
in her coat pockets, clues to help him
face what's left. All he can do is walk

early mornings through a world gone strange.
From sinister bushes birds trill odd calls,
as his fingers curl around

crumpled tissues, bits that mark
his private tangle
as the sun's first rays strike.

Stone Soup

I. *Arturo in Watts*

The pond was still until I dropped lettuce and earthworms on
its surface. Then koi rose, glittering like Kazuko's tiara when
she waved from a pick-up festooned with flowers, the Strawberry
Queen. I was the scrawny boy she didn't notice in the crowd. Two
weeks later a military truck hauled her family to Manzanar. I
wanted her to return to find her fish grown, each scale magnified,
more brilliant than she remembered. I wanted her to know what
the powerless can do for one another.

II. *Kazuko in San Francisco*

My first job after camp was in an office high rise. I could see
down into the piano store where Dad bought the upright we had
to leave behind. My boss left loose diamonds scattered across his
desk. He would pick one at random, absently rub numbers tattooed
on his forearm as he lost himself in the gem scope's enlargement
of angular facts. He wanted hot coffee, a secretary who hungered
more for Mozart than for stones. Each week I cashed my paycheck,
dropped dollars into a jar hidden behind my icebox. When they
reached the rim, I bought a used piano.

III. *Stone on a desk*

I've been prised from settings,
sewn into coat linings
time and again. Beneath anxiety
each owner brings what she's kept hidden
among the carrots and potatoes
of her dreams. Her eye
makes me a pool

to cast a wish into.
My clarity isn't emptiness.
I flicker with light.

The Lost Woman of San Nicolas

No one saw me slip over the rail
until I was already swimming home
to save myself from missionaries
who planned to save our tribe.
Wave-slapped, I saw their ship
tack toward the mainland, my parents
shrieking as I disappeared from view.

Eighteen years later, I stand on this ship
watching my whalebone fence shrink
to a white dot on the bluff.
For weeks I hoisted ribs up from the beach
to plant in a semi-circle before my cave,
points curving outward.
Onto them I carved my effigies.
Women scraping otter skins, laughing
and slyly judging each other.
Men posturing by fire
or seated, chipping obsidian
into spear points.

Often wild dogs skulked and growled
outside my fence. But within
my inside-out whale, I could consider
what I needed to be:
a man-spirit who fashioned tools, hunted.
A woman who used sinew to stitch
cormorant feathers into a cape
becoming sometimes the bird itself—
draped in feathers I'd pace the cliffs,
peering out to sea.

When I spot this ship, it simply means
a transition. I'm ready to go now.
My family, so long imagined,
brushes the air by my shoulders.
I'll be taken, as they were, to missionaries
who will offer me a dusty courtyard
to sweep each morning and give me
tuberculosis. The mission padre will record
that I was the last speaker of my language
and never learned his.

Why bother?
Father Gonzales has no words
for who I am on this day

before he clothes me as one of his own.
My island reduced to a smear on the horizon,
I lean against a cold brass rail.
Breasts bare for the last time,
my cape flutters and shakes
back to the wheeling sea birds
iridescent wings.

Consulting a Mayan Calendar

When I can no longer hear voices
filter down from the night
and stars no longer seem the coat
of a mythic beast, I lose the signs

that tell me where I am.
For direction I look into a hand mirror
lying face up on the bathroom counter
to see myself as I am seen

by those who gaze up
from the soil. They see first
my soles, then above my head
the planets' iridescent trails.

They see me looking down
holding my own gaze
until I find a flicker
of what the jaguar knows

when she wakes at dusk.
She listens as wind maps her path
to the river. Even as she laps
the night's first water

she does not look down.
She senses the nerve
of the north star above her.
She focuses ahead.

Hard Fruit

(Based on a tale from the Tzotzíl of Zinacantán)

He fakes sleep as his wife's head floats
over their blue agave fence
of juice and thorns. The rumors are true—

her head leaves her body each night
to sleep with someone else. Furious, he rubs
salt on her severed neck

then waits for dawn when she quietly
tries to clamp onto her torso
but can't. Furious, she fastens her head

to her husband's neck, screams
how could you do this to me?
and bites his fingers when he tries

to slap her off. He has no choice. He has to work
two-headed, his wife spitting
obscenities in his ear as his bicycle wobbles

down the dirt road to the *mercado*, headless
chickens tied by their feet to the handlebars.
Business is slow. Customers stare

and buy their chickens a few stalls down.
Sickened, he unwraps tortillas anyway,
feeds her bites, his wife chewing, grim

and glad that when she shits
it's through his anus. Finally, after many failures
he tricks her head into fastening onto

a deer's rump where, skewered by branches,
it drops and dies, a hard fruit he buries
beneath her favorite tree, the sapodilla, papery brown

skin of its fruits fluttering around him
as he prays each evening to escape the pit
in his stomach, the chill against his throat.

Rain Makers

A red glitter candle twinkles near the tip jar,
the bartender's talisman of heat and balance
as she pours another kamikaze.
A little buzzed herself, she senses
the raincoats draped over chairs, steaming.

And from the open mouths on the dance floor
she thinks she sees the breath they exhale.
Even the harmonica clamped in the guitarist's lips
blasts wet notes and from his microphone
damp moans rise. A collective humidity

wafts past the bouncer perched on his stool,
past the smokers on the sidewalk
where scrambled voices join the snores of drifters
curled in doorways, the controlled release of roshis
in late night meditation, the pure exhales

of daffodils and elms. Molecule by molecule
breaths recombine and rise,
muffling the night sky with clouds,
gathering together liquid weight
for their exhilarating fall.

Postcard, Ten Years Later

Prague was overcast.
You thought you saw my overcoat
crest an arched bridge
then cross the cobblestone street.
In Sevilla, a quiet afternoon.
Geraniums. The courtyard pillar
you lean against as you would a friend
becomes a waist in the curve of your hand.
A faint breeze that suggests
my scent—sage and a river mouth
of damp Pacific sand.

The Wait

Penelope's lovers
are never mentioned—
they're symptoms, merely
of her life, its daily raveling.
If a stable boy's muscled leg
resembles her husband's
it matters only to her, only for the hour
she holds him, looking away
to fill herself
before he assumes
the shape of any other husk,
as she does, the next day.

Into Laertes' shroud she weaves
patterns of an ordinary life,
the accumulations
denied her—a first sour kiss
on waking together, or
late in the kitchen,
everyone else asleep,
the cups of wine they would have
bent over, knees touching,
voices quiet.

She closes her eyes to relax
into the soothing
she never mistakes
for communion—
candles, a bowl of water
a young man insists
on sponging over her pubic hair
to watch curls rise
like sea urchins after tide
sluices away.

Odysseus, in his travels, recognized love
either as flesh or vague memory.
After years of athletic
writhing with sprites and witches
he barely remembers human pulse
matching his own belly's
rhythm. In truth, he'd been relieved
to be called by duty
away from the bed where,
after lovemaking,
nervousness stirred him—
uncertain he could return the length
of Penelope's bold gaze.

But he returns home certain,
by wits and guts, he has unknotted
the thickest mysteries to cluster
the Aegean, a houseful
of would-be usurpers
adventure's last demand. Safely bolted
behind an oak door,
Penelope hears the riot begin.
Crafty and bent, she finally smiles
up from her loom.

Siri Says

When you see the poet
who has forgotten the word *leaf*

picking up leaves from her lawn
one at a time, pause. Say good morning

for the gift of her wan smile.
Scan forward. In two blocks

a drunk will stumble and glare
as though you made him forget

how to breathe. Walk 200 feet then
answer your cell. Tell your lover

about the lost people, your shared good fortune.
When he responds Whatever

look straight up. Above the elms
sandhill cranes fly north.

Take a breath. Siri says
you can still change course.

Blow a Kiss

I. *Mata Hari*

Men smoke in safe shadows,
watch the hypnotic drop of veils

until my oiled hips and V of hair
glow in plain sight,
the secret they want most

revealed. Outside they long for
the courage to air each treasure
they've been given.

Here they inhale
the scents of another country,
imagine a culture

where each truth is shared.
Palms up, I welcome them in.

II. *The German Officer*

My chest constricts in staff meetings
where facts choke my lungs.

Even at home when I taste
the brine and frill of my wife,
the moment passes too quickly.

I long for an exhale, for secrets
to swirl out past my teeth,

Jonah through the whale's mouth
back into the sea.

III. *The French Soldier*

Rifle raised, I aim for her heart,
but just before she's blindfolded

she spots me, knows
I'm like the others, a man

who longs for the slip and heat
of bodies.

My commander gives the count
and she whisks off her blindfold,

blows me a kiss. When my bullets
open her chest, she stains the wall

and looks as though
she could be any of us.

Afterlife

Parachute silks rustle and fold as you thump down.
Weight them with a rock, no need to recycle here.
Follow mariachi music down the hill
through crazy yellow field mustard.
A woman gathering laundry from a line
will see you pass and abandon her chore,
place shirts in a wicker basket
then smooth her hair. A fisherman
will fold his string of trout into an ice chest
and walk to meet you, offering you a swig
from his thermos of whiskey and hot tea.

They heard you were coming. Main Street is festooned
with crepe paper flowers and a fragrant *mole* simmers
on someone's stove. The town folk are setting up
picnic tables in the city park, telling jokes
as their missteps and regrets from the other world
fall away. What matters is your arrival,
strolling to the tune of guitars and birdsong
as everyone stands—the orphan, the shepherd,
the mariner—all with glasses of chilled wine
raised to toast your safe landing.

Toshiko Takaezu's Closed-Mouth Vase

If there's an accident—the vase shatters—
three or four shards will reveal words

scored with a stylus before Takaezu
pinched the mouth closed.

One might read *spring*,
a fragment in the alluvial scatter.

The artist, a woman of these times,
thought ahead. She reminds the stricken owner

that even an irreplaceable world
offers tidings from the wet clay of its creation

hidden until the old form breaks open.

III

Alebrije

When I met his eyes
and stroked his finely-sanded

wooden belly painted leaf-green,
I sensed a frog-shaped hole in my torso

empty all my life. Now my *alebrije*
perches on my nightstand

and I no longer fear the descent
into dream. His amphibian smile leads me

across the grass-rope bridge strung over
a river gorge. I trust my dream feet

on slick cables because he knows water
and grip. His back is speckled

like cottonwood duff alighting on ponds
and like all mystery

is multihued so I can spot him
even in murky water as he leads me

through shallows and reeds up the path
to a hole in willow bark, a nest

where I curl, slow my breath,
my heartbeat, awaiting the new.

Courtland, California

It's grown so dark
we must climb by touch
the riverbank embedded with 2 x 4's,
half ladder, half stairway,
to reach the levee road.

At the top we brush dust
from each other's jackets.
The party's shut down and our hostess
stretches out to sleep
inside her creaking houseboat.

By now your wife sleeps too.
So you pause, sounding
the low notes of my name
as you point to a sky
gently split, then opened, the stars
seeds we lift our faces toward.

On the land side, tree tops of a pear orchard
rustle at eye level.
If we slid down the bank
we might walk slowly, then together
pause before a trunk twisted
to a make-shift altar.

We might leave what we could find
in our pockets—pennies, a ticket stub,
offerings for what we only notice
at odd angles in half-light. But my gaze
would descend, then, from the hollow
of your neck to your shirt's simple buttons.

So we don't slide down. Instead,
we hold each other for hours
in conversation on this dirt
packed to protect the orchard
from the river's seasonal surge.

I'm home by 2 am, alone.
Dust sifts from my shoes
onto the clean kitchen floor.
From my coat pocket I draw a Bartlett,
slicing it in half to inhale
the fragrance of wet soil
and honey, to see the vein stretched
between the seeds, keeping each alive
in its own fleshy cloister.

Steam

Of course he never called back.
But what surprises me
is how his bathtub materializes
at the far end of grocery aisles,
behind the bank teller's window—
his legs draped over mine,
the way he reached above us
to trace my name
in the steamy mirror, just to watch
the letters disappear.

The Driver's Seat

We weave through cars and semi's
bent forward, me trying to melt

into his back, lean
as he leans, my will sliced

by 90 mph wind. Any shift can throw us
sliding across the freeway, so I pray

to trust his reflexes, pray
to careen down the exit ramp

into silky residential streets,
to his bedroom

where he rolls a skinny and inhales,
features lit. I watch his half-closed eyes

and think about my car, just outside,
the key in my pocket.

Sustenance

I.

Stan taught me salt, the way he learned
  from YouTube—first stand sticks in shallow waves

then beyond the tangled line of seaweed.
  When they dried, he ran his fingers down,

seeking to feel his fingertips crystalline,
  almost First Nation.

This is how they preserved food, he said. In winter,
  small bites of dried venison, smoky with ocean aftertaste.

II.

George taught me smoke: soaked hickory chips
  sprinkled on charcoal. He aimed a water pistol

at grease fire flares and placed his non-filter
  between my lips for the first toasty puff.

We sat on the porch steps with a beer and I closed my eyes against sting
  swirling through hibachi vents, closed my eyes

as he leaned into my hair and inhaled,
  transfixed by fire's fragrance. Before he left

I learned to sear a crust on flesh,
  let coals cool to ash.

III.

Simon, years later, simmered garden vegetables
      then slid overboiled carrots and peppers into the trash

with a shocking lack of guilt. He poured broth into jars
      and stored them in my freezer. We didn't last the season

but months later, alone, I thawed a jar
      and sipped broth from a mug, savoring

the lessons I saved for myself, each man
      still within me, making me strong.

Newlywed

Alone in an ice house tidied with wallpaper
and rented cheap off-season,
I imagined the former tenants: ice blocks.

For hours I studied Betty Crocker's
gingham-print cookbook and practiced
waiting for my husband

by brushing sand and more sand
off the mattress. Through afternoons
I walked empty streets

keen to spy behind closed curtains
the sextants and compasses
nailed to walls, reduced to relic

as sea wind scoured porches and eaves.
I was nineteen and didn't know artists
begin in places like this.

Compass

It's go time. Your dust-coated Peterbilt
edges from the chute as cattle shoulder
one another and low, settling in for
the ride. Fighting sleep, you call me

to talk, keep you crisp. On the old paper
map I keep open the weeks you're gone, I
find the highway town where you fuel, a dot
on a line, and from there trace the back roads

around Wyoming scales, imagining
your stops at ranches and feedlots. Our cell
phones are miracles. My voice reaches through
your exhaustion until you say your eyes

can focus. The road is clear and you can
picture it now, our kitchen table, home.

Weeding the Cosmos

I read myself into picture books of myth,
a woman who spins cloth and hunts wild boar,
until the day my body broke open
in childbirth. One week later I curled on my side

nursing our newborn while my husband
rubbed himself against my haunches.
Then I saw myself as an instrument
for others, my skin a balloon
for silence.

My story should turn here,
the woman gathers herself, speaks up,
but in that moment I sensed
my original sisters across the globe—
one in Uruguay, another in Burundi—
each one rubbing a husband's shoulders,
braiding a daughter's hair,
dreaming herself in a story where a woman
hikes alone through wilderness
armed with her folktales.

I try to meet their hard acceptance
of what's real. I've grown into a woman
who can chop down jasmine with no remorse
though it's scented like a princess.
Its woody stem will be shredded,
turned into the soil, just as
my own body still has its uses.

Like women everywhere, I tend the growing
and the dying. Shovel in hand,
kneeling among spindly flowers
I know *woman* as constellation,
the base of my spine one star,
the crown of my head another,
a gardener weeding the cosmos.

Christmas Concert

The parents enter exhausted, ears ringing
with the evening commute, with radio news

of bombs in Kabul and campus gunfire
one town over. Even among sparkly cardboard bells

each thinks ahead to a fast food dinner
then bills, then laundry.

Then the curtain stutters open. A third-grader
runs to the piano, arches his hands and plays

Pachelbel's canon in D, notes chosen over 300 years ago
still true. The adults shift and raise eyebrows—

surprisingly good—he's like their own kids, noticed
mostly in fed-up swats and after-bath cuddle.

When did he learn to wait for end notes
to fade into prayer?

Next, a chubby, messy girl walks onstage.
Mid-December, she wears navy-blue shorts

bunched at the crotch and stares at some back corner
to focus, to project her voice in tones so pure

adult smirks freeze. Somewhere outside
the stars are brightly shining

and the audience stills, listening
as she sings a nearly forgotten secret,

as though she is the winter secret
whose breath exhales promise.

Jack and the Beanstalk

She won't apologize for shouting
but packs a lunch for his climb

then waits below to throw him an ax,
shocked by the giant who falls and flattens

their wheat field. Second shock: Giant's blood
plumps the wheat kernels

she harvests and grinds for daily bread
that's darker, more moist than before.

At each meal she studies her boy.
No longer starved, he grows taller

and each day more inclined
to gaze past her. Jack studies

the clouds as he chews, sotto voce
humming the songs he heard among them.

Edge

I descend the Dipsea Trail to the wavering seam
where Mt. Tamalpais grass becomes seaweed.

A red-tailed hawk hovers at eye level,
ruffled by wind that casts invisible seeds,

some drifting to soil, others to salt water,
my lab results still one day away.

Time to follow the old code, plant a feather
for luck, for the quiet minutes

before my doctor enters the exam room,
the news tamped down within

his lab coat, his hunched shoulders.
He will open the file and begin to speak.

Attack Ships Off the Shoulder of Orion

(Blade Runner, 1982)

Roy bestows on his last witness
those ships and c-beams glittering,
two images that were his alone

until he saw his own death
closing in. Less stoic
than Deckard, I blink through the sweat

of 3 am whiskey shots
to listen as you fast-talk,
frame by frame

cowhand scenes that make you say,
Couldn't kill me with a pickax.
You reach for the bottle

and I picture the smash
when a desert mustang bucked you
into the corral fence,

the sweet gamey aroma
of cow shit and sage
you close your eyes to smell again.

You say, *A man can't drown
if he was born to hang,*
then reveal that tests

confirm an expiration date
hardwired in your DNA.
You're talking like you want me

to absorb the sunrise you saw alone
on horseback, snow-coated cattle
glowing orange. I'm high and open

to receive that light, to wince
at each rib broken, each cut healed,
seeing now I'll escape

alone to solid ground, unable
to retell all you gave me
on this crumbling ledge.

Ride the Invisible Thermals Up

My love never touched bottom.
He sank away from his beloved
nasturtiums and rows of green beans,
away from his guitar
shoved under the bed. Sank so low
he fell right through bottom
and into air again, his body left
to formaldehyde, eyelids stitched shut
for one last look
before he was wheeled into fire
then sealed in a clear plastic bag,
ash and bone bits.

Love, fistful of ash
I hold you again, release you
again, a toss into surf.
Our last touch is you
under my nails, grit in my teeth,
the wind through my hair
dusty then clean.
You're here now in sea grass blown flat
by salt wind, in the burnt
twist of driftwood I bring home
to place near our sweet peas, climbers
like you now. Trapped for so long,
you've slipped the sickened animal
you'd become and return to me
in our garden, in guitar notes
that slip through the radio,

our open window. Homesick James
strums and I almost hear again
the tune you wrote

for the family we'd become,
notes that drifted each evening
through our room. Listening
I can almost feel you enter
my lungs as breath, slip away
as notes that scatter and ride
the invisible thermals up.

Hush-a-bye

Sandstone crumbles in each boy's grip
as they scramble up a seam

of the Death Valley crater we've hiked into.
My thin shouts stop them and they turn,

still tethered to what voice
a single parent can muster,

sliding back down against sandblasting
January wind. Now they're safe, buckled in.

I drive the White Mountains, catch in peripheral vision
a moonlit wash spiked with cactus

then a sudden gorge. My job is to sing,
breathing in rhythm as I hit

the sharps and flats of lullabies
and scout ahead for black ice.

Blue-Bellied Lizard at Divide Meadow

When my shadow falls close the lizard flexes
and puffs her turquoise neck, switching a thin new tail
that stretches from what was once a tail-stump.

Thistles grow in dozens where the meadow stops,
green stars, purple sprays of stickers.
The lizard must see a prickly forest

but I can ignore what's before me
to envision a single thistle sketched in a book
precise and whole, then dissected to quarters

and finally the sex drawn alone,
an illustration of the human need to divide,
measure pieces. My favorite book describes

Tu Wan who, in 12th century China, divided stones
into categories to sort the fantastic
from the ordinary.

He'd travel great distances to see
one shaped like a tortoise
or a horse, and would take notes

separating color from luminance.
As a final step he'd strike
a stone with a small brass gong

to hear the stone's unlikely voice
rise to a clear, high pitch.
The lizard, too, retrieves the unlikely.

She must scurry, then freeze to balance
the cool tingle of the ghost tail
with the heat of this one growing through it.

I kneel to watch her tail-tip sweep, collecting
more sensations than she thought she'd lost—
splinters must seem sharper now

that she anticipates their sting,
but too, in the fine soil under this mesquite
she might find silkiness in a world that last year seemed

all teeth and edges. According to his records,
Tu Wan collected hundreds of stones
he later called useless. Most he stored in a cellar

but he kept smaller ones in his house to weight
paper, hold open doors. One day, by mistake
he knocked from his desk a persimmon-shaped one,

a damp blue-black. It broke, exposing a central cavity
in which a little fish jumped about,
convulsing in light and air

as it died. Tu Wan gasped and scooped it
into his palm. With one fingertip he brushed
what he had no category for

and held the fish closer
to examine its scales—
how nearly invisible, how slippery.

Grown and Gone

I wash the walls of this quirky home
like women wash gravestones, tending
the presence of loved ones

they no longer touch. Fingerprints fade
while I daydream a narrow forest behind the plaster,
all wooden frame and frizzy electric wire.

Outside these walls in distant cities
my sons live their own elliptical paths
around the sun. Electricity threads

from their heads to mine. Quiet mostly
and then a spark. They're vibrant
as the Chinese pistache outside the window

flickering yellows and reds. Autumn
shines the room, almost liquid,
and rinses the silence alive.

Lepidopterist of Closet Moths

(After Roger Reeves and Ocean Vuong)

Someday I'll love Lisa
just that much

before the name of a father
or a husband. I'll lose my expertise

in self-denigration,
a lepidopterist of closet moths,

every mistake
pinned and labeled.

For decades I've studied
their coppery wings.

Lisa, your tweezers
and magnifying glass no longer

reveal surprise. It's time
to close the glass lid

on your collection
and try something new.

Trace circles in a sand tray,
begin the mental walk

between granite and obsidian
back to the Ur-girl.

Remember, before you wished yourself
bride or mother, before you became

this crimped scientist
you were a bony child pedaling uphill

past your playground by the cemetery
at dusk. Lisa, she is still you

fully yin and yang, the lit spokes of your bicycle
spinning. Feel yourself again

as you were—though evening deepens
and headstones begin to glow,

pull up on your handlebars, stand on the pedals
and pump hard for the crest.

Thanks To

My heartfelt thanks to Randy White and Josh McKinney, two remarkable writers who read my work closely, cheered me on, and suggested changes that made this collection stronger.

Most of these poems grew under the guidance of two writing families. One is the Redwings—Victoria Dalkey, Catherine French, Carol Frith, Susan Kelly-DeWitt, Kathleen Lynch, Mary Zeppa, and the late Quinton Duval. The other family is Catherine French, Denise Platt Lichtig, and Gary Short. All of these incredible poets give me bracingly honest feedback and unconditional encouragement in my efforts to grow as a writer. Years after my official studies with him ended, I am still guided by the artistry and humanity of Dennis Schmitz.

I am also grateful for close friends and extended family who uplift me, always. Finally, thanks to my immediate family: Paul, Jack, Jackie, Andrew, and Gracie—your wisdom and humor sustain me.

Acknowledgments

Some of these poems have appeared in the following publications, and grateful acknowledgement is made to their editors.

Cumberland River Review: "Christmas Concert," "Handmade Gifts"
Cosumnes River Journal: "Think Back"
Hardpan: "Rain Makers"
Mobius: The Journal of Social Change: "Stone Soup"
North American Review: "Grown and Gone"
Poet Lore: "Blue-Bellied Lizard at Divide Meadow"
Poetry East: "Afterlife"
Prairie Schooner: "Emigration," "Postcard, Ten Years Later," "The Lost Woman of San Nicolas"
Southern Review: "Jack and the Beanstalk"
Sow's Ear Poetry Review: "Edge"
Suisun Valley Review: "Closure," "Lepidopterist of Closet Moths," "The Driver's Seat," "Seamstress," "Steam," "Sustenance"
Tertulia Magazine: "Hard Fruit," "Passing Through"
Quarterly West: "The Wait"

Note: Some of these pieces were published with different titles or in slightly different versions, and a few appeared under my former married name. Some poems in this collection were published in chapbooks by Red Wing Press and Swan Scythe Press.

About cover artist Monica Aissa Martinez

Monica Aissa Martinez has exhibited widely in museums and galleries including Nothing in Stasis: A Solo Exhibition at the University of Arizona College of Medicine; Between Earth and Sky: Contemporary Art from the American Southwest in China; the ASU Art Museum, Drawing with Everything, Phoenix Sky Harbor International Airport Museum, Connections to the Natural World, LA Artcore Brewery Annex, Los Angeles and notably State of the Art: Discovering American Art Now, Crystal Bridges Museum, Bentonville, AR. Her work is also found in private collections throughout the country.

She lives in Phoenix, Arizona with her husband and their cat and teaches drawing at Phoenix College. She spent last summer as Artist-in-Residence, researching Alzheimer's Disease, at the Tempe Center for the Arts. More of her work can be seen at: http://monicaaissamartinez.com and https://monicaaissamartinez.wordpress.com

The cover art is titled *Coyotl - Urban Coyote*, and is 26x41, casein and egg tempera on canvas. Regarding this painting the artist writes:

"The body, human and animal, is like a landscape of intricate structures, complex and full of variety. It's a whole organization, made up of systems and connecting parts. I find it all beautiful and poetic. As I go from shape-to-shape, work-to-work, I find myself searching deep within the nooks and crannies. Where is its source? Is there a narrative?

I live in the heart of the city. I read that people are spotting coyotes in my neighborhood. I sent notice to the wind that I wanted to experience one directly. We'd already caught one on video walking along our front lawn. The wind did not let me down. A few days later, on an early morning run, a coyote crossed my path. We looked at each other. It moved slow and graceful. I return to the studio and begin preparing canvas."

About the Author

Lisa Dominguez Abraham lives in Sacramento, California, and teaches at Cosumnes River College. She won the 2016 Swan Scythe Chapbook Contest for *Mata Hari Blows a Kiss* and both a Bazzanella and A Room of Her Own Award literary award from California State University, Sacramento. Her first chapbook, *Low Notes*, was published by Red Wing Press in 2007. Her poems have appeared in journals such as *Southern Review, Prairie Schooner, North American Review, Poetry East, The Cumberland River Review, Tule Review* and *Mobius: The Journal of Social Change*, among others. In Spring 2018, she was the featured writer in *Suisun Valley Review*.

She is also involved in community activities involving art and poetry, participating in the "body stories" series by the Sacramento Center for Contemporary Art, based on the work of mixed-media and video artists koo kyung sook and Sandra Davis, and writing and performing "Respite" in response to Wayne Thiebaud's "Flood Waters" as part of the Crocker Art Museum exhibition "Wayne Thiebaud: The Homecoming." Most recently, she wrote "Disguise" to accompany painter Frank Ordaz's "Stella" for the Sacramento Metropolitan Arts Commission's "In Response: Poets & Artists in Dialogue." The poem and painting are now a sign and mural in the Auburn, California, Central Square Art Park.

Blue Oak Press Literature Series

The Blue Oak Literature Series embraces the breadth of culture, ethnicity and geography of the American West by publishing and promoting works by both new and established writers and poets.

Eileen Curtis	*Girl on a Mountain*
William Everson	*The Mate-Flight of Eagles*
James B. Hall	*The Art and Craft of the Short Story*
Bill Hotchkiss	*Dionysian Chants from Woodpecker Ravine*
Bill Hotchkiss	*Fever in the Earth*
Bill Hotchkiss	*Jeffers*
Bill Hotchkiss	*Middle Fork Canyon*
Bill Hotchkiss	*The Graces of Fire and Other Poems*
Bill Hotchkiss	*To Christ, Dionysus, Odin*
Robinson Jeffers	*The Women at Point Sur*
K'os Naahaabii	*Curios of K'os Naahaabii*
K'os Naahaabii	*Notes from the Center of the Earth*
K'os Naahaabii	*The Bitter Roots of Peace*
A. M. Petersen	*Stars in Twilight and Other Poems*
Judith Shears	*New Leaves*
Edith Snow	*Hold Your Hands to the Earth*
Edith Snow	*The Water Mill*
Edith Snow	*The Good Yield*
Edith Snow	*Winter Tree*
Randy White	*Motherlode / La Veta Madre*
Randy White	*Blood Transparencies*
Lisa Dominguez Abraham	*Coyote Logic*
Pos Moua	*Karst Mountains Will Bloom*

A Note on the Type

The text of this book was set in elegant Centaur, the only typeface designed by Bruce Rodgers (1870–1957), the well-known American book designer. Rodgers based his design on the roman face cut by Nicolas Jenson in 1470 for his Oxford Bible. The italic used to accompany Centaur is Arrighi based on the chancery face used by Lodovico degli Arrighi in 1524.